Miracle Marks

Miracle Marks

Poems

Purvi Shah

Curbstone Books / Northwestern University Press
Evanston, Illinois

Curbstone Books
Northwestern University Press
www.nupress.northwestern.edu

Printed in the United States of America

10 9 8 7 6 5 4 3 2 1

ISBN 978-0-8101-4038-7 (paper)
ISBN 978-0-8101-4039-4 (ebook)

Library of Congress Cataloging-in-Publication Data

Names: Shah, Purvi, author.
Title: Miracle marks : poems / Purvi Shah.
Description: Evanston, Illinois : Curbstone Books / Northwestern University
    Press, 2019.
Identifiers: LCCN 2018059564| ISBN 9780810140387 (trade paper : alk. paper) |
    ISBN 9780810140394 (e-book)
Subjects: LCSH: Women—Social conditions—Poetry.
Classification: LCC PS3619.H348 M57 2019 | DDC 811.6—dc23
LC record available at https://lccn.loc.gov/2018059564

For my tributaries:

Sharda Ba and Manek Dada for educating generations of girls & emboldening a lineage of feisty women — including my mother, Bharti Shah

Saraswati Ba and Natwar Dada for my father — Kirit Shah, a fountain of caring

Every sisterhood & collective flowing towards justice

CONTENTS

Tributary

Tinder

Gust

Loam

Language & Lila: (Re)marks

Tributary

The poet enters the game

Black blood
of a star: bent
      light

or as we say —
woman.

❁

                  — music
coming from afar   or within

            & you know not.

❁

Skirts flaring:

      miniatures —

circles of ardor, fertility

   of glances —

❁

Chances. Your dance as
      misplaced   — laughter &

         blue wrists where
               your troubles
return into a praise, echo

saint's song —

❁

                  Mira says my marriage
was a scandal. My love   never was.

❁

        You

spy a silver
flute seducing

      sorrows and prefer
your own drum, devotion

as an alphabet without a final

letter.

❁

Women astonish you.
And then you
become one.

Beating her soiled clothes, Saraswati reaches God and bursts into tears

In Hinduism the first menstruation of a young girl is a cause for celebration, with special presents given. However menstrual blood has generally been considered impure. At my grandmother's house, women were not permitted to cook in the kitchen, had different utensils, ate and slept separately. They were also not allowed to enter the prayer room. Nonetheless, when as a 12-year-old girl I visited my grandparents during the summer holidays, my loving and pragmatic grandmother spared me this embarrassment by asking me to not tell anyone about my periods!

— KUMKUM BHATIA, "Why can't girls enter temples during menstruation?," *South Asian Parent*

Where the river pulls off red
                            veil or living

            shroud, a tiger sparks
in woman's breast. When no one

is watching, the tiger learns
to swim. It follows the river   as river makes

as if there were no day nor night, no moons to keep mark. The river has nowhere
to be, no one to carry, no fabric to fold, no births to assume, no opinion to praise, no red
blotches to whiten, no sleep to solitaire, nowhere to hide sore breasts, no need to compete

                                                            the black cloud
                                                    for lavish rains, nowhere

        to go as it is always going there — there   always going — absorbing

curd of sea, absorbing salts off a girl's thigh, blood
off a woman's smile.   Forgive your smeared

compound, lair
for your cramp

scrap, piles for
everything that is

usable, this stack
of your own   future limbs. You want

                              the power to turn

a trident into a spoon, your hand
as the first cup from which a toddler

drinks.   You
               believe
                                        you can

       talk to river, calm it down, reason it. *Woman,*

have you not   learned?
You may birth   your ruler.

                                                        You feel every

destination but perfection in this lifetime, your sore
                    skin as moon origin, as bountiful

                                        contamination.

At river's gather —   clumped fabrics
of you.   Measure: 21 feet. Measure: 27   feet.

                                        These waters,

               how they bear   scar

rings, tried
wombs, incarnations
that could never be

seen.

                                        After encountering

               tiger, I spun my destiny

                    as only water can — moving without

       moving, being without breaking

                    whole. My lifetimes

are prowling

since this river

conceived. Women rip
around me, keening longings,

tiding

hopes. Mark

the streaks of my salvation:

these spilled wants   come apart,

come home.

Mark the blood of my limbs: once they   were river   too.

The way you have folded laundry, Saraswati folds continents

Her relationship with her husband strained apparently beyond repair, a 27-year-old woman drowned her two children — a six-year-old daughter in a washing machine and an 11-month-old son in a bucket — and then committed suicide at her home.
— "Mom drowns kids in washing machine, kills self," *Hindustan Times,* June 6, 2013

A monsoon born. She lays   out a sari

of lakes molting. She hums the first   lullaby
she ever heard. Can you caress   sunset? Your clothes

refuse to fold symmetrically. They have too many stories
to be squared & tucked away.   Each curve

of a woman's throat is drizzle, each reverie   rumpled
rains born as breast. Water can shape your   skin

the way your regrets tide your beliefs.   You want
to be more than mantle, a man's   public.

Such secrets can only
be captured   by rope,
topography of rungs
ascending heaven as dark
seas birthed. Flattened

against a floor, our scars
yet stick out.   As you lengthen

          knots, you pray your soul
                    has found a new river

the way you hope

                              no daughter

is ever stuck in this machine we call a home:

each compromise
an unbirthing,

each argument a dry
        shore, ribs

before prayer.   May you each

        now have new bodies   with new relations   knowing

                continents move

through lifetimes, that once-   river provided   dancing ground, sisters

        chattering secrets, dark anemone swimming through our veins. Ache

            is a memory   of ocean.

Today, hope

the laundry
is dry, stacked
neat, your children
playing.

Fear only what tomorrow does not bring, the sorrows you never got to hold.

Maya knows how the day walks carrying heartbeats

Resurrect flesh

as rivers:

Ask who unwombed

you. *Question* your own

creator. Learn

the rules. Understand mystique

as *beyond*.

Flicker *empirical*. Collect

signatures.

Drum these selves

in dust & *borders of wars*.

Speak through boom as if you *have a choice*.

Saraswati praises your name even when you have no choice

Patel, a 33-year-old woman who lives in Indiana, was accused of feticide — specifically, illegally inducing her own abortion — and accused of having a baby whom she allowed to die. The facts supporting each count are murky, but a jury convicted Patel . . . she was sentenced to 20 years in prison.
— EMILY BAZELON, "Purvi Patel Could Be Just the Beginning," *The New York Times Magazine*,
    April 1, 2015

You had a name no one
could hold between their

      teeth. So they pronounced
  a sentence. Had you the choice,

you would pilgrim
to the Vermilion. It is no

Ganges, but you could dream for tiger's
      blood, for eight tributaries to open

into palms bearing girls unfettered. Before your baby

was a baby,   could it float? Could
a stillness of breath   be the air asking

for alchemy   as you cast your life as a spell? These days
the world is looking   for witches. You had been

searching for an hour   beyond labor, option

of pleasure, a choice unscripted
by parents, borders unscripted

by choices, a passing
salvation. You had not

expected this state — punishment
for a wrung womb. These days

you mourn: when   you are free, you won't
be able to bear   the children you

wanted. In silence, you pronounce   your name as if it came
from the crucible of river, from the first   throat broken

                    into a cobra of desiccated streams.

Mira pulls a fish out from the banks of the Jamuna

The ocean of rebirth sweeps up all beings hard, / Pulls them into its cold-running, fierce, implacable currents. / Giridhara, your name is the raft, the one safe-passage over. / Take me quickly.
— MIRABAI (translated by Jane Hirshfield)

You know a fish thrown on the bank does not go on breathing.
— MIRABAI (translated by Robert Bly)

Flails in her hands, dark

with back & forths, so many

from one. She touches protestations —

sour memoirs/wracked pleasures — bequeaths

the ache of constant   swimming — eyes

bulging

towards air, scales absorbing

each stroke —   & yet this one is unready

to be held. In touching,

she knows a beloved.

Back into the river she throws

the quivering thing — until

it is ready to be taken whole.

Maya offers light to an absent reality

Unsung tale: your soul.

Sound the glisten.

      Re-living: old soul.
        Old soul: re-living.

Consider response between a wave &
          a particle, the difference

     between living as repetition
and *repetition* as living.

     The space between

         this verse
       re-versed, *undone* —

        where your spirit

                lit

open,

         surrendered — less

          pulse than *hum.*

Saraswati works water, hums generations

Worldwide, women and girls spend an estimated 200 million hours — daily — collecting water . . . "Just imagine — those 200 million hours add up to 8.3 million days, or more than 22,800 years," says UNICEF's Global Head of Water, Sanitation and Hygiene Sanjay Wijesekera. "It's as if a woman started with her empty bucket in the Stone Age and didn't arrive home with water until 2018."
— MALCOLM G. FARLEY, "How Long Does It Take to Get Water? For Aysha, Eight Hours a Day," *UNICEF USA*, March 1, 2018

Each day, your water tank
                overflows. Motor

                        running, mind forgotten, clamor

of reminiscences, roar
                of a husband past, buzzless
                        bungalow now left

to manage, to occupy, to mark   as your own.   Each day   surprise

      captivates: you, 85 and still newly single — 70 years
of spilled news as marriage. Through wet stones, you hear wives'

tales & chant. Behind that, you burn, caged ocean   as tremor.

❀
A sea away, I hear
        murmurs. Legacy
                or premonitions, my
                      own longings

for a home to hold, a body

        to hold, stillness or waters

                as meditation, as births
                    for which we are still

praising.

❋

You seek to turn a door into a gate, unhinge
a frame to make it a ladder — how you climb

up to the tank to coax
water's pinched drip, how

you climb

        & rest there on the ledge, gazing out, looking upon the near stars —

                or your neighbors — or your own gnarled hands —   or nothing — at all.

❋

With four daughters, it's near a handful. That missing
        son, a bent thumb, another iron gate to cross.

❋

You mortar flour into breads & marvel: did the emperors
erect arches, gate upon gate, to welcome the city or to keep us

out? Did they build their private wells as some girls
trudged villages to rummage a pot of starving

                      rivers? You know not. The bread

rises, round, almost its own stomach,
      a gnawing   patient to give birth.

❋

Forget the spilling
tank. Forget
the risen breads. I want

to learn horses, how
to ride gust, bear

ancestors through my hair, shatter

every dwelling into dispatches on a hero's quest, fill the well
of our longings with visions of surrender, a self never in need

of repair.

❀

Skin

compels a world   between waters.
Every expectation   boiled.

You slice an onion and see

Columbus's breach, how exodus   can bring you nearer

to where you ought to be, this next

world you are still working   to —

❀

                Savor. Indoors, you dream.

    In the dusk, you pass
        a peacock feather

through my fingers —

resilience   travels   lifetimes, shaking

   hunters & colonizations — utterance

      as bouquet, revolution of heartbreaks.

❀

In mornings, you petition

creation.

❀

    — wick

      struck — a gulmohar fallen from a tree older than you — how you kneel
to pick its fruit, how a bud graces earth across dearth. How

your visions of life & death are like the walls of your own heart, pumping, bifurcating,

              relentlessly congregating.

*

The value of water even before
                    a cyclone.

The value of women even
before the public sphere.

The value of a bed before
                    it is dusk, before you need

to make it home with the day's wash or sloshing pots or tomorrow's tank.

                                                                How we live

for lineage, grains to mouths, spills to plenty, women to women.   How we live,

as a lamp in service
            of being lit.

                                        How we live, replenishing
what we have spilled with day's making, cupping darks, sieving what we have

                            into a smaller

        tank, into space of   wanting for not & not

                                        wanting for — boundless

reservoir of our wantonly spilled dreams.

Maya appraises what to do with all your stray emotions

Store music —
first rainbow struck pale. *Shoot*

all the mynahs

in your melodious

eyelashes. Nourishment is banter, a self
as querulous exotic. You do not

know the converse of plenty. Threshold: grocery
of marigolds & vermilions. Our touch

surfaces from darkness. *Your hum*

beside me: just another way to say
sorry. *Black geyser* crumbling.

Precision of an inexact proportion. Your arm

gesticulates, furious & loyal as harvest. What
you never remarked but *already* relinquished. *Perfect*

is a syllable for *absence.*

Saraswati marks lineage of the missing

The United Nations estimates nearly 200 million girls around the world are "missing."
— CORTNEY O'BRIEN, "Did You Know 200 Million Girls are 'Missing'?," *Townhall*,
September 22, 2013

I have known a grandmother and two have known me.

                                                                You search
for missing limb, reveal a tree with disparate pattern of branches — one side

whistling, the other   — accordions of leaves. You expect a thinning
          at the top but wonder if this tree feels terribly bruised, a woman

with half her hair, a woman blistering   bald-

sense in wild stutter.   Lineage often skips
a relation. You search for an ancestor. In your dreams,

a daughter travels. She wakes you when
          you need to rise, kindles in your skin
scent of the tea she is about to brew. Another
          journeys with you on a crowded road, haggling
with the vegetable-seller for a better rate. She has gotten

so wise in so few years. Some mothers count off

years on a ruler against a white wall, children growing shoulders & span
of necks. If you could mark your unmade memories, every black wall would need

altars: room   now for praise.   A mythical river can spawn

          civilizations
                    but can a mythical girl civilize? You tell

one story and hope it survives.

A young girl holds a subway door
for an old Chinese man who needs

a few more steps to reach. The girl

                       says, *Do not mind your battered*

      wings. The peregrine nearly
    became extinct: chemicals singing

        generations.   So you move

       around your pain — from
            a womb
    to a shoulder, you float

across aerial silks. You pacific

                sky. She

says, *now the peregrines are returning.*

           Fury keeps

      a river
        invisible.

              You bruise
      a ventricle or chafe
        a throat as you recover soar, a realm
            where every elbow
has room. Pain is temporary. Flight is not.

You see trees shedding leaves you never saw they bore.

You observe girls sleeping in the missing river.

    Shhhhhh: do not wake them. You may disturb dreams,
                birthing.

You take out your ruler & in the unseen waters
                — notch   each body, growing.

Saraswati nods to the white man who, after hearing her liberation poems, embroiders "dowry"

Even now, goddesses

outlast colonialism.

Tinder

This is the truth:
As from a fire aflame
thousands of sparks
come forth.

— MUNDAKA UPANISHAD

(translated by Juan Mascaró)

The poet enters the game of lila

There is an old Sanskrit word, Lila (Leela), which means play. Richer than our word, it means divine play, the play of creation and destruction and re-creation, the folding and unfolding of the cosmos.
— STEPHEN NACHMANOVITCH, *Free Play: Improvisation in Life and Art*

    Mud as if you are
        being made & the mud is too. In dead

        bed of quenched river, you see

          a tiger's eye, graffiti
            across every hearth
        barred to girls, a swami's shed
          skin, rows of tanks

seeking a water
source, blue

mountains of
ancestors.

❀

           Saraswati raises
      her bangle — a stream

    spills into empty frames, sudden
      gossip of girls at a summer

pool, clarinets chirping.

❀

      Your bangle, wet
        with absences,

   churns

      more stories

than our stars themselves.

❁

Your bedroom mirror goes dark.

Too many rivers with new
names.

❁

You hear the voices of women who never
drowned, who could actually
never be

drowned. You touch
your skin and mark

a ghost, perhaps
too many to count.

Saraswati dozes, two hands as a pillow beneath her head

I was seven years old when I first saw a Sacred Thread ceremony. As a girl, I was jealous of the attention and numerous gifts that were being showered upon my nine-year-old brother. What bothered me most was that my brother got to learn the Gayathri Mantra--the supreme and most sacred of all Hindu mantras, which is the basis of all other mantras and the essence of the Vedas . . . I didn't get to learn the mantra . . . The father teaches his son the Gayathri Mantra under a dhoti, which is spread out like a tent. It's whispered by the father into his son's ears. To my brother, the mantra was an opportunity to tease his little sister. Each time I asked him what they had told him, he would give me a mischievous smile and tell me "a secret."
— VISI TILAK, "A Hindu Bar Mitzvah," *Beliefnet*

Noise of her bangle at night. Secrets
the days, whispers surprise to sunrise.

Caresses your arm as one's mother once did.   Glimmer,
if not sleep or Saturn's rings,   can be its own reward. Dreaming feels too long, skin
                                                                                    drifting

                              as song. She pauses:

                              can secrecy be a sound? She believes morning skillet
          is underside of the sun, her breath is nest and bird, sister Gayatri yet

a jewel of some snoring sadhu's dream-drowse. The glass jars vibrate

with beads & unpopped seeds — such unstruck belonging. From her feet
                              to gut to throat, from wrist to shoulder to ear, she hears

murmurs, the tremors of one verse unspiraling, elongating,   recycling night

into night into night   into night.

At the edge of her bangle, Saraswati reckons with the one flame

The very mentioning of Hindu sacred thread ceremony (Upanayan), a Vedic practice, for
a girl or woman will cause a flutter among orthodox Hindus and traditionalists. For the
conservatives, sacred thread ceremony is only for boys and men. But Sejal Amod Ketkar,
eight-year-old girl from Thane, went through the sacred initiation rite and the ceremony was
performed by a female priest as male priests were not ready to perform the ritual on a girl.
— ABHILASH RAJENDRAN, "Hindu Sacred Thread Ceremony (Upanayan) for Girl Child —
Breaking Traditions for Good," *Hindu Blog*, May 29, 2009

Is fire not pure?

First, anoint me black

> bangle shimmering
> in the glint of a girl's
> wit & raised head. Second:
> adorn

your shoulder as though you never burnished thread.   Third: do not attest
just the to-be-men had claim to   flame. Darken infinity —

our wrist horizon — let sunrise remind

                                        us of a match

at the household altar — how these marble
gods tender at our everyday's grace. With

a fistful

of grains,
crocus, neem

leaves & a blanket
of marigold slivers,

        blaze

our dreams upright, perfect that circle

      of sacred
      flesh, seek

      succor

      in round sound
      of metal to metal,

two hands clinking wrists, two hands
marking story & history, two hands
dancing creation & its return. After

such reckoning, blossom

    then child, string resonance,
unbend circle, spark alphabets

in the air, filigree syllables as fierce
mettle — sound your fiery god

                -praise.

Mira — as lit — through a triangle — of encircled wrist

In one glint of jagged sun — throws of bangles.

These round sound-glisteners are worn
        so you shall announce my arrival, so you shall

offer me never-ending song. Murmuring
        my desires, mine & yours, yours

    or mine, they clink   as triangles touched

      together —
         in your
      curved ears

distant dreams nearing — nearing distant dreams.

    When they knock — mirrors meeting — silver
      laughter — lustrous
         ghosts — lips —
               — gazeboed — our

      inner door   — cracks —   wide.

                    Moon

                      flung &

                shadow
             as light's
          strand,
      spun &
          revealed & —

—

            sky-born   shrines.

                Here: find

face. Here:
        yourself

in one geometric glance, not quite cloud
crystallized, not quite worship's window —

            but then
    were you to bring   here

          your hand   to your lips, as if you

          were eating sound, as if you were

          eating light, pealing my slowly spilt

skin — as if you were round
    near round & round were through
        me now — stroking   the greatest
          prayer —   as murmur — as   — revolution —
                as   — light.

Saraswati waits for silk & turns to cotton

It is however widely believed that some of the Vedic chants' vibrations are so powerful in nature that once a woman starts chanting those regularly, she is likely to lose her femininity and get masculine characteristics in both appearance and psyche.
— HAREKRISHNA S V

        Dark correspondences — yes/yes — summoned
into these bedrooms of your throat. Dark

        limbs lava-limbered — a bloom
                        of hollows. Where

is our seamstress? Before cotton, you sought

silk — gripped
        song. As day,

this too dissolves, leaving only

molt, a used holy
thread & 108 webs

of murmur   as butterfly
        broth   to be burst

through thick canals. You   echo & re-echo a verse
the chosen repeat   at day, mid-day, end day. Let

now your praise cocoon. Skin
now your breasts' chrysalis. Tremor
now your throat's carapace: let such

ruth

of cotton trouble you —

memory & dark making.

Mira marks how dark can unveil blush

Even in the dark, you mirror.   Spark —

                                        widow remembering
                              her wild web, wallflower

that sang as if a chorus
had come. In such dusk,

you have traveled. Yes, with you,

                                        I have traveled.

                              Did you only   mark

haze —

scab —

bite —

                    of our partition?   Attent

now your coal-spun cheek/   night-scour

        for shared day. Bring   your compass, your compact, your curious,

                                        your own hurt
                    ember   to stoke or summon

flame. In your clamor-

dinned dark, in your
tawny rungs, in your

mesmerizing blacks,
in you —   my

open blaze.

Mira seeks to unpuzzle warmth

When you speak, a star tremors. It remembers

its own light. It seeks

to send you a signal, vary its cadence — ask you.

You eclipse/you sojourn.

Fingers beckon rub:

rapture/
vibration

burst
clang
clatter — —

skirt of fires

Maya sees purity is false passion

                                        We curdle —

    you crave quick thicket of fire, a lip stroke against
tendon, a sweetness singed sweeter. *Rain comes*
                                                & goes. You churn
                        succulence,

            dissolve limbs, dark
            of *reciprocation* —

    your own
            incense

                    palpable.

    Your skin learns
to clarify monsoon, *distill*

more than one *burn* —

                    evaporate wholeness from inside the flame.

Maya incarnates the phoenix

You pursue *trail of dust*. Oil
gulped by cranes, a sea graced

                                        by ash-fault. You travel
                            to cool yourself down.

            One path — survival —

                    within

                            your two

                                legs,
                    the seams
of a caterpillar, the curves
of an almost monarch.

                                Dust & dust
                            is a matter

of discernment. You descend

a staircase, bark
of former forests, each step
            splinter
            & cabin.

You were born
                            with fire
        inside you. You

were born
to be re-born. Husks

migrate

nerves

undress

— disintegration

as your first
self.

Mira inspects her forehead & offers a genesis

Where you touched me, there is a hole.

                                        Now then — a comet
                                                circles

its own tail, swirling prayer
        for keepsakes — kindling   limbs

                                with crumpled requests — stalling
                imminence for illumination —   who

strikes such thirst
        that is neither   hum

nor burn, just

                                        blackness we
                                                breathe —
                                                —

Gust

yogaś citta-vṛtti-nirodhaḥ
— Patañjali, Yoga Sūtra 1.2
(*Yoga* is the stilling of the changing states of the mind.
— translated by Edwin F. Bryant)

pramāṇa-viparyaya-vikalpa-nidrā-smṛtayaḥ
— Patañjali, Yoga Sūtra 1.6
([These five *vṛttis are*] right knowledge, error, imagination,
sleep, and memory.
— translated by Edwin F. Bryant)

The poet enters the game of lila & marks

There is an old Sanskrit word, Lila (Leela), which means play. Richer than our word, it means divine play, the play of creation and destruction and re-creation, the folding and unfolding of the cosmos. Lila, free and deep, is both delight and enjoyment of this moment, and the play of God.
— STEPHEN NACHMANOVITCH, *Free Play: Improvisation in Life and Art*

Divinity works
through distance.   Maya chuckles

as you wink   your good

            eye — you never

  meant to gamble
                but then life —

✿
You are
still

trying to figure
if you want

        to find your way

✿
So
you are

still
a third

rail —

Your palm sizzles —

Maya admits there are two or more protagonists in this story

Your mind.

Maya speculates if — at this time — this is —(indeed)— the right train to — right now — board

Sometimes *you believe you*
are at the correct   *station.*

And then you discover

                                        the station

is about to close permanently, that yours
        is the final   train to go forward   in this moment: You

            hunt   for followers as bolster   should you slip

along journey: You
consider joining   another moment — impossibility

            sliced as *option*: You persist —
        envision yourself as pioneer   in *retrospect*: As *last halt*, you
                            will claim   you

                                        are
                                    your own best

station:

travel a million inflammations   just to be   in your own   skin —

                                    embrace original   solace.

Amongst the disappearing crowds except this ruthless rail

in your head, some

voice

provokes
that every journey is

taken solo. All else is illusion,
mad piston or liberation, hopeless

belonging or brethren of star matters. Now or again, now or
then, in time or out of time, in station or out, either

you or the crowd
carries/propels: *Go in any direction, but go.*

On the platform, Maya troubles *Arrest*

Station: *direction*

      makes you drowsy. Too many

options or too few, a knee catch
      as in *rainy weather may come*, the slant

of sky before assured storm. If I were to tender
         all the wisdom of movement, a tornado

would twist to dust & the *swoosh-woosh* of bandits'
      yelps careen to koel-calls under banyan.

We all expect   *something stolen.*

      You go one way — I another.

Across the tracks — you divine
      a face & feel   pleased

by presence, *knowing desire*
      hovers &

      gnaws, knowing

sticky skin & perfume — what
your prayer's dark mark in one

incense or indissoluble

      exhale — *arrests*. Our mystery

as appeal.

Maya — on the brink of transferring — to the express

                                        A sharing beyond

                            sense: part
                            ineffable, part —

                            ininscribable. The train
                            is waiting for me — across

the platform. From *zamana*, you count backwards in hopes

            of reaching *zero*. My people invented   this nothing. My people invented

this mark, *round journey*
of here & return. Yours, each tremble

                                    that follows/
                                            precedes.

The train — is waiting for me across the platform.

                                        Fervors. Dreaming
                                                of night

                            jasmine, cord of glories
                            in every dawn. We each tend

a *fertile home*   — one   we'd like to make
our world   in forfeit   of hand-scarred labor.

                            The train is waiting — for me across the platform.

Without you, a half.   No whole, therefore, without
        you.

The train is — waiting for me across the platform.

                                        Chatter of susurration: a song runs
                                            your head, portends drum, opens

                            oud's thrum. You fail at the lyrics

but then had you known them —   ever? Had you ever
        known this world in the salt of your fisted heart? Some

                                    become part of memory without

entering knowledge. Today you want to carve

these disparate jars of your brain — logic

                                or creativity, fact or fiction — rewire
                            loose circuits, snip certain memories & yes,

morsels of knowing too — these sonatas of birds basking
wind, this sun serenading sleepless eyes, your hand

        ample against my hip —   *you could bear losing these too.*

        Here the train is — waiting — for me across the platform.

Across the platform, for me

                                            the train is waiting.

Across the platform, the train   for me, is waiting.

Maya lies awake,
        invoking an old flame

Have you ever

dreamt how subtle night

is? How *breath's* rustle

varies our *gravity*?

How the moon turns

mortal, bringer-
of-illusions spent,

first love's shadow, ever —

have you

embered?

Another village passes.

On the top bunk, I surrender sleep.

Maya marks a destination

From stallion's eyes, they were

meadows, restless

sweeps

of cud, congregation

of runaways

chasing —

endless track.

Except you had been there & there & there & beckoned *I follow*

where I'd find you basking   in the moment, awaiting

nothing but the sight

of my sight.

Maya marvels what it would be like to have her Self meet herself

Perhaps a series of ghost   rails or a *shadow* —

Perhaps a chain of wrecked   *conversations* —

When she again gestures   to the window, *we all*

wonder, what does

                                        she?

Maya challenges you to a staring contest

Her jilted heart, *waiting*

for someone to gaze

rapt as a

sprawling fan on a Southern

porch, *each self bent* out

of shape, absent & kinetic

as you or my own

— eyelash

you *almost flickered*.

Loam

And within the body, a vast market —
Go there and trade,
sell yourself for a profit you can't spend.
—MIRABAI, "Mira the Barterer"
(translated by Jane Hirshfield)

The poet enters the game of lila & marks a number

There is an old Sanskrit word, Lila (Leela), which means play. Richer than our word, it means divine play, the play of creation and destruction and re-creation, the folding and unfolding of the cosmos. Lila, free and deep, is both delight and enjoyment of this moment, and the play of God. It also means love.
— STEPHEN NACHMANOVITCH, *Free Play: Improvisation in Life and Art*

In some accounts, you
are not even you.

❀

Memory must be made before   it can be erased.

❀

                              Mark:

some ancestors I have   chosen & some have chosen me. I came

                                        from the East — as you attest — in
                    a lyric to the West.

❀

Witness:

                    sparrows crushed
          from migrations,
                              bangle of black
               pulse, a train's hum —
                                        nestled
                    at the curve of your lumbar

a once silk,

                                                  opening.

57

Saraswati says in my name, love the sweet of yourself

India's government is advising pregnant women to avoid all meat, eggs and lusty thoughts.
— Nirmala George, "India's no-meat, no-lust advice for pregnant women ridiculed," *Associated Press*, June 20, 2017

Stating that she will "request" the Central government to hang people who eat beef as "status symbol", Sadhvi Saraswati, from Chhindwara in Madhya Pradesh, on Wednesday urged Hindus to stock arms at home to "save our women from love jihad".
— SMITA NAIR, "Govt should hang people who eat beef: Sadhvi in Goa," *The Indian Express*, June 15, 2017

Woman, do not eat last.

❀

Women are not
meat, though women
are treated less
tenderly.

❀

Woman, do not love last.

❀

Women are not meat unless
they are treated as food
for men and the sons growing
                inside them.

❀

Woman, do not worship last.

❀

Women are not meat, though women
carrying meat have been harmed.

False
saints need protection
through
falsehoods.

❀

Woman, do not lust last.

❀

The sensation

of a hand against your spine even
as you grow another spine inside

your belly. Only union can tell
you of unions. Only harmony

can tell you of harmonies. How

would the world know itself
otherwise? Drop the arms

in your arms: bear
vina — such

arms are worth
my name, sweet water

pot pitched to pour

songs and spring
ecstasies. Love the river

of her that courses into you. Love
the river of her   that courses into you.

In the 21st century, Mira remarks — Krishna's ways of loving belong in a parallel universe

And when you promise me your heart,

        will you banish   the flock

of cowherders, the bevy of skirts & dangling chains

        which traipse
          in your shadow?

    I am still

learning how the wide chest broadens, how   the ample heart

can find its own edges, squeeze
thin borders against lung & ribs, this universe

      of opening, remaking & mortaring a room

        for blossoming.

Such allowance for love is not as natural as crawling   or even singing, though
       we prize

its music over many others — sometimes as hymn, sometimes
as dirge, sometimes as sometimes —   the whisper

barely heard.   What awaits you?

Reach in then and grab hearth but first   jettison flute
lest   we both

meet sorrow before each other,   the wind of night & sigh

of branches beginning   to drip dew, beginning

to shake with wettening   exhilaration. This universe

is ready. Tell me —   are you?

As she writes sky —

                                    cosmos in a graffiti
                                              nozzle.

From the lips of high rises, a girl
who could have been architect

                                              etches world. On each conked out
                                              window, she dawns wishes, carving

                        swans & accordions & gust through
                  every depressed beam. Never empty

            are her inks — feast
      emerging from all the untenable places

our gods deserted. How does she dazzle

            that corner of brick so far from
                                    ledge or window?   Clouds jostle

      restlessly, shoving

inscriptions through sky. She whisks night
aside: a moon crosses the battered

mansion of her hands. She

                        will not reveal mystery

as the frantic traffic cop, stomach roaring, salutes
her enigmas, motions pedestrians scan higher, value

hawk's eye. Saraswati
knows distant dreams

can bring appetite, gnawings stubborn
as skins. Your fists provide a banquet

                of universes banging through turmeric
        palms.

                        A revolution

completes — Saraswati's tools now cloaked. In your hands, a plate
        pauses. When you look into the face

of God, you are hungry. Come
then, eat. The dish is set: saffron

              to footprint your dreams
        traceable, marigolds to distract

      the other girls & even the lower
   gods, thick milk to beget thirst, fistful

of stain, yes, this entire village   sings.

Mira longs to be more than a bride

The sound of your footsteps

is waterfall. Why not thrust
        off these bangles then? You

                            are already music & in your hands, I am

wordless sound in your worldless sound. Note this

concert of veils rising & fires
        crossing. A palanquin came
                to witness how my head adorned
                        by marigold can bow, can summon

                                        rich timbres of dawn — how night consorts

with day to disappear, how we thrum

a single pulse —
twins

        in a mother's pouch, both their own
                              & not own
                                    — our original
                        unchambered heart.

I shall wear the moon

or your heartbeat
                only
around my wrist.

Maya shuffles plates, hoping to generate electricity

She despairs that lukewarm icebox, rank of singed
wood, that thick of kerosene. She wants to drink

shade. She wants to hold the substance
of your hand. *She wants not*   to want.

Sometimes rotation is progress, sometimes *the illusion*
of progress — revolution *free of charge*. Maya

is tired of illusions. *She wants to eat.*

She wants to generate. So Maya serves

variables, *quirky* & new: All
we have is today. [Today is code

                        for this moment.] All this moment
                        has is *memory of your voice*, a lapsed

            proton (such potential). Ah, this world

            — *lingering at beauty's edge* for one
strong force   to break air from

gravity, time   from space/collide shadow & self   manifest

            —*charge.*

Mira unfurls her hair into a bell when — from this ringing — mirror emerges

Such dark lip of the beloved

        in swirl of untangled
              strand,
      revealed.

Here: a mirror's
             black
     obsidian,

             spark

unspooled from earth's
   throbbing.

                 Core: your heart

            bore origin
              here.
                 Shaken,
        see mantle

    scattering,

                your fingers clamoring —

                    eruptions

in each thumb's stroke.   Tresses

tremble —   unshorn

              delights,

              — promisings &
      divinations.   Listen

to the peal   of bloom   in your mouth.

                                        You land

at nape of neck, cupping this struck spilling
        into your shuddering

hands, arcing your lips
        into the darkest

fountain, finding here trill

        & original light, finding here

that which first brought you —   your own sight.

Upon catching snatches — of you — fastening strands of a woman's

                                        hair — the finest
                        locket —

                more electric
                        than breath along neck —

prank of a perfect harvest

                        dark pulse
                                honeycombed
        — questions'
                buzz — Mira

razors   her own
        black

case.

When promise disappears, Mira speaks to the thorns

Sorrow: may you be known
        by your other names — black

orchid, a scar burst, a thorn
        at your jaw, the underbelly
                of ecstasy.

Sorrow: were you to have a season, should you be
        lodged against a cornered tiger & my raven

throat? Sorrow: may you fall
        between autumn & winter or extreme

beauty & extreme quiet or
        extreme bliss & extreme plenty, between
        a burnt blessing & its thorns —

or ideally between Sunday & Sunday,   a day of day deleted. After raptures,

beloved-talk, a smile
        in early light, how easy a heart

betrays, how each & every nerve
        re-speaks splendors —   lost. So we turn

back to the same dilemma,   joy more slippery

in the hand & somehow
        always
        & in each
        season   sorrow standing

for your shoulder — perched

to draw blood.

Saraswati — rendering — between sparrows

Every house shares a haunting. You smell

       childhood waiting to fly away.

❀

The police lights do not respond to the raised voices in the wall. Neither do you.

❀

You have opened foreign banks, off-shoring
       memories, believing your own songs
are unremarkable: small, narrow, unworthy.

In your closets, bullied
selves melting. You navigate
mythologies as if they could be —

❀

       — as if the story is just beginning — or if in the blink
of an eye — you missed all the vital parts — perhaps even

your only way home.

❀

Call &
       trill & call
       & trill & call
           & relent

& you wish . . .

❀

You know not the names
       of birds serenading

your walls.

You have begun

surveying from your glass to the church raising
        its steeple as a fist, this keen beak at your back. You move

between sparrows: curtain

                & flight, transcendence & nameless, haunting & home.

❀

Sometimes

        a bed tastes of   island: how two can enter

from split shores, how conversation

                feathers   your rooms
                                                        of hope — notes hemming

                                        or heaters
                                                whirring,
                                        gathering
                                                        their secrets
                        before blowing steam.

❀

A signature, a voice.

❀

When the bedroom plaster parts, clusters
of dried bruise — your tongue remembers
                its time as a wing.

Maya entices you to reach out & touch lightning

Palm against palm.

Keep lifelines, scars, constellations —   go

                    now:

                                        discharge

          fate.
                                   Brand inscrutable,
                                                            kindle
                              what you have
                    always

          feared,
                    what in your hands, you have

always *known*.

Mira barters infinity to raise her hand

In deserts, I discovered —
rivers, in this one

moon — seas without

water — your perch
on a worn

mountain, shaved
road   of our

reunions, hurly-
burly of a village

we have both

visited & longed

to blaze

— this mirror of my palm

held as something

once
divine.

The poet enters the game of lila & marks a number of miracles

*There is an old Sanskrit word, Lila (Leela), which means play. Richer than our word,
it means divine play, the play of creation and destruction and re-creation, the folding
and unfolding of the cosmos. Lila, free and deep, is both delight and enjoyment of this
moment, and the play of God. It also means love. Lila may be the simplest thing there is
— spontaneous, childish, disarming. But as we grow and experience the complexities of life,
it may also be the most difficult and hard won achievement imaginable, and its coming to
fruition is a kind of homecoming to our true selves.*
— STEPHEN NACHMANOVITCH, *Free Play: Improvisation in Life and Art*

✿

> You board the train, leaving Maya
> behind. She always catches up
>
> to you, ready to share your next
> adventure before you have lived

it. Every express is

> an illusion & heartbeat — the nearest

✿

prospect for —

error

✿

> or as marked through the rear

mirror: miracle.

Language & Lila: (Re)marks

In many places, surviving birth as a girl child is a miracle.

Everywhere, a girl is a miracle mark.

❀

My mother is the eldest of four daughters. In a sonless house, my grandparents in India, who came from villages to the city, educated all their daughters. While neighbors called my mother and masis "stones," my grandfather called his daughters "my diamonds."

❀

How are women marked? What marks do women make? What does it mean to be a woman? What does it mean to be? Sometimes it's the questions that are the quest in the quest for liberation.

Sometimes it's the poetry that tenders space to make mark, dance creation.

Liberation — shared.

❀

Typography is a lila (play & *playing*). Mira, Saraswati, and Maya as interplay: readers/*listeners* move across figures and form constellations, make connections, embody worlds.

Space for revelations — for feeling — for being — for decolonizing our selves.

Reader as resonance, language as bodies — sharing. A dance/creation.

❀

In the United States, Hinduism is known derivatively — through writers such as Henry David Thoreau or Allen Ginsberg or Elizabeth Gilbert — or via Western yoga. How can we further liberation from the inside, offer space for critique as well as subjectivity without centering Orientalisms?

Or a translation: how do we keep spirit while critiquing capitalism from within capitalism?
Or Hinduism as a Hindu?
Or America as an American?

❀

Hum of love & labors.

Reckonings of sufferings.

Also: praise. Our stories, vibrations of survivals.

✽

And with so many girls denied access to education, writing by women is a miracle. A miracle mark.

I come from this lineage, grateful to have been taught English — my immigrant language — early and to be a writer.

Writing in English is already a betrayal of the ancestors.

And a victory.

✽

Language is an ancestor. Language is energy. Sound is being and an essence of transformation.

As creation, as the evocation of Shakti, poetry is a body of the feminine divine.

A ceremony of creation, inquiry, queer wonders, transformative energy.

These poems beckon you to dance with them, play the page. Together we create ritual.

Play of the divine, play of divinity. Lila.

✽

In the umbra of misogyny, racism, xenophobia, and all structural oppressions, how do we re-constellate our sacred space? How do we render our multiple realities? How does our poetry bear witness and foster liberation?

Perhaps through darpan of dialogue and healing — reflection, community, action — towards equity, towards transformation.

✽

The poems speak for themselves though they do not speak for me. At least not always.

✽

I worry about the colonialisms of experience, how we as women of color distrust our experiences. Are made to distrust our experiences. Our felt wisdoms. This wisdom in the body — across bodies.

Knowing moves across us, my words cross page — a decolonization of movement, of expected lyric, the spaces we can occupy. Migration as spiritual practice.

✿

How does karma interact with systemic oppression?
What is chance? What is luck?
How does karma take into account social body? Actions that are forced? Or limited choices?
Power dynamics? How do we link collective good and change?

Chance of it. Chant of it. Circles as spirals, evolving justice, evolving lila.

✿

Sometimes the poems do speak for me. In these times, I worry about the rise of Hindu fundamentalism, the paradox of goddesses and femicide, the shrinking democracy here and there. How to wrestle with oppressions of our making/in our names, how to re-mark, how to create space, spur justice for all. Stand against purity politics, communalism, casteism, homophobia, white supremacy and colonization in all its incarnations.

✿

I seek to re-claim the dark and the feminine divine as holy.

✿

My grandmothers — both of them — were named variations of Saraswati, our goddess of arts and learning.

I am the first artist I know of in my immigrant family. Perhaps it is luck or perhaps it is the natural bloom from branches that brought me to being.

✿

How do we embrace the corporeal and cosmic body?

✿

My grandfather prodded my grandmother to take classes after she birthed my mother. My Ba, who had a fifth-grade education, a new baby (my mother) to care for, completed evening classes in order to get a seventh-grade certificate. The cost of nurturing, the costs of freedom.

Each of their four daughters earned a college degree. I earned a Master's.

The cost of this language here, the blossoms my grandparents could never have expected.

✿

How can we all get more free? Together.

✿

You will not find them but the traces are here: Sita's flames, the textures of Draupadi, the holy dark of Kali (and also Krishna).

❀

Language is migration.

❀

As a girl, I devoured books. Sometimes my white teachers were threatened by me. Sometimes they put me in my place — the place they decided for me. For many years, as an immigrant girl, I did not know, did not feel — I could take up space.

Poetry is a taking up of space, a questioning of gaze, a marking of our labors, a making space towards liberation.

❀

Against violences, erasures, cooptations.

Rites of passage for all. Learning for all.

To feel breath in language requires migration of sounds, requires rooms for opening — space.

Requires desire. Possible selves. Magics of living.

❀

Water is a flow of sounds.

Women's blood is the life waters of the world.

❀

Beyond relatability, can writing evoke curiosity and story-sharing? What rituals of womanhood are experienced in your communities? What does the texture of devotion feel like? How do you taste longing? What does it mean to be a woman when so often we are told how to be? What is the horizon of being beyond gender?

❀

Question inequity. Embody sacred.

Call. Respond. Dance, create, live in the *parallels*.

❀

I've called. I've rung. Will you play?

ACKNOWLEDGMENTS

Acknowledgment is gratefully made to the journals, presses, or websites in which these poems, at times in different versions, originally appeared.

"At the edge of her bangle, Saraswati reckons with the one flame," *Belladonna**

"Beating her soiled clothes, Saraswati reaches God and bursts into tears," *South Dakota Review*

"In the 21st century, Mira remarks — Krishna's ways of loving belong in a parallel universe," *Quiddity*

"Maya admits there are two or more protagonists in this story," *Belladonna**

"Maya challenges you to a staring contest," *Barzakh*

"Maya knows how the day walks carrying heartbeats," *Southern Women's Review*

"Maya shuffles plates, hoping to generate electricity," *Southern Women's Review*

"Maya — on the brink of transferring — to the express," *Toe Good Poetry*

"Mira — as lit — through a triangle — of encircled wrist," *Barzakh*

"Mira longs to be more than a bride," *Four Way Review*

"Mira pulls a fish out from the banks of the Jamuna," *PEN America Journal*

"Mira seeks to unpuzzle warmth," *Barzakh*

"Mira unfurls her hair into a bell when — from this ringing — mirror emerges," *One Pause*

"Saraswati dozes, two hands as a pillow beneath her head," *South Dakota Review*

"Saraswati nods to the white man who, after hearing her liberation poems, embroiders 'dowry'," *Barzakh*

"Saraswati praises your name even when you have no choice," *Split This Rock*

"Saraswati — rendering — between sparrows," *South Dakota Review*

"Saraswati waits for silk & turns to cotton," *Belladonna**

"The way you have folded laundry, Saraswati folds continents," *PEN America Journal*

"Upon catching snatches — of you — fastening strands of a woman's hair," *Belladonna**

"When promise disappears, Mira speaks to the thorns," *Four Way Review*

GRATITUDE

Miracle Marks emerges out of the cocoon of community.

The first poems in this collection were written in 2008. I am grateful to my beloved community who has — over this last decade — enabled me to create art, share it with the world, and relish in possibilities.

I offer praise & open-hearted thanks to:

* the Jerome Foundation for a Travel & Study grant which enabled me to spend time immersing in Sanskrit chants & dwelling in sound energy

* Belladonna* Collaborative, and especially Saretta Morgan, for publishing *Dark Lip of the Beloved — Sound Your Fiery God-Praise*, a precursor chaplet to this book

* Jen Bervin, guide, soul-whisperer, and facilitator for our 2013 Emerging Poets Fellowship with rock-star poets Mahogany L. Browne, Jessica Elsaesser, Paul Hlava, Rosamond S. King, Elsbeth Pancrazi, Montana Ray, Andrew Seguin, Eugenia Semjonova, and Ocean Vuong. Profound gratitude to Elsbeth, Jessica, Mahogany, and the brilliant Jen for your deep, affirming, and generative feedback of early versions of this manuscript. Props to the team at Poets House including Joe Fritsch, Reggie Harris, Stephen Motika, and Lee Briccetti for making the fellowship (and this book!) possible

* Eduardo C. Corral for your always generosity in the Writing Across Cultures workshop and to fellow poets Miguel Angeles, Aziza Barnes, Mahogany L. Browne, Amanda Calderon, Paul Hlava, Sarah Key, Benjamin Krusling, Ansley Moon, Saretta Morgan, Timothy Ree, and Jenny Xie: thanks for your kindling & kindred. A big heart shout-out to Nicole Sealey and the fab folks at Cave Canem for sharing liberations

* the wondrous, soul-bright folk at Kundiman and particularly the rock-star *Together We Are New York* crew: Hossannah Asuncion, Tamiko Beyer, Marlon Esguerra, April Naoko Heck, Eugenia Leigh, Bushra Rehman, Zohra Saed, and R. A. Villanueva

* the Sheyr Jangi rabble-rousers who make every lyrical battle a delight: Majda Gama, Rami Karim, Aurora Masum-Javed, Sahar Muradi, Sham-e-Ali Nayeem, and Zohra Saed

* the luminous duo of Raquel Almazan and Mariana Carreño-King alongside my cohort at INKTank: Oscar Cabrera, Liz Morgan, and Cynthia Robinson. And to Monet Hurst-Mendoza and Nancy Kim at Rising Circle for always bringing forth delights

* NURTUREart as well as the Lower Manhattan Cultural Council Workspace program (and especially Bora Kim) for giving me space. Anjali Deshmukh, artist and friend-sister extraordinaire, for helping me take & make space in all the ways – including with our Make Your Self Meek/Make Your Self Vast & lila collaborations

* Molly Rideout and the Grin City Collective for furthering public art, and to my fellow artist trouble-brewers, Keva Fawkes and Anna Swanson. A special shout-out to the staff and patrons of Burling, Cedar Falls, and Marshalltown libraries for inspiring my poems and showcasing them on your library windows!

* the Asian Pacific Institute on Gender-Based Violence, Manavi, and Sakhi for South Asian Women for giving space to my poems during anti-violence convenings and vigils

* organizations including the Asian American Arts Alliance, Asian American Writers' Workshop, Brooklyn Poets, Jus Punjabi Radio, Lincoln Center Out of Doors, Metropolitan Museum of Art, The Poetry Project, South Asian Magazine for Action and Reflection, South Asian Women's Creative Collective, Split This Rock, and VIDA Women in Literary Arts — for amplifying my voice

* the inspiring folks at the Asian Pacific Institute on Gender-Based Violence, Casa de Esperanza, Center for Court Innovation, Center for Racial Justice in Education, New York City Mayor's Office to End Domestic and Gender-Based Violence, and Women of Color Network, Inc. for enabling me to further an art of change

* my desi somatics crew for having my back: Pooja Gehi, Soniya Munshi, Bhavana Nancherla, Deesha Narichania, and Yashna Maya Padamsee

* my fellow artists and writers without whom this work could not be, including Gabrielle Civil, Aditi Dhruv, Sarah Hartzell, Mona Hazeur, Madhu Kaza, Maggie Messitt, Sue O'Hara, Lyn Rajguru, Sarika Seth, and Sejal Shah; my XXCalibur playmates: Dacyl Acevedo, Ogonnaya Dotson-Newman, Samia Khan, Nancy Kim, Tina Lee, Adeeba Rana, Seema Sabnani; and, artist Nandini Chirimar for a seed of collaboration that spurred this book

* Jill Lisette Petty, who came as a miracle and continues to be a wonder: words cannot express my gratitude for what you do & who you are

* to the whole Northwestern University Press team, thank you for making home for me: this book is our shared lila

* my whole family, and especially the folks without whom none of this is possible: my parents, Bharti & Kirit Shah.

Thank you all for the miracles — shared.